WICKED
GEORDIE
ENGLISH

WICKED
GEORDIE
ENGLISH

DIANA BRISCOE

Michael O'Mara Humour

First published in Great Britain in 2003 by
Michael O'Mara Books Limited
9 Lion Yard
Tremadoc Road
London SW4 7NQ

A CIP catalogue record for this book is available from the British Library

ISBN 1-85479-342-X

1 3 5 7 9 10 8 6 4 2

Designed and typeset by Design 23

www.mombooks.com

Printed and bound in Great Britain by Cox & Wyman, Reading, Berkshire

Introduction

If you find yourself in Tyneside, Durham, Northumberland and especially Newcastle, in the north-east of England good manners may prevent you from saying of your hostess – 'She's kizzened the pot' ('She's burnt the food') and hopefully you will never need to ask 'Wull yi luk me heed for dickies?' ('Will you please delouse me?')! But you may find it useful to know that the correct response to 'What fettle tha day?' ('How are you?') is 'Nowt but canny' ('Very well thank you').

Nobody knows for sure where the word 'Geordie' comes from, although theories are manifold. One possibility is that the word came from the name for a lamp invented by George Stephenson in 1815 and used in mining, which was then used for the miners themselves and, eventually, for north-easterners in general. Another theory is that the name derives from the time of the Jacobite Rebellion of 1745, when the people of Newcastle and the surrounding areas were on the side of King George, and therefore 'for George', which eventually evolved into 'Geordie'.

The 'Geordie' accent is unique to the area and this

book concentrates on regional words and pronunciation. Many of the words derive from the traditional occupantions of fishing and coal-mining. It has a lilting tone, perhaps due to the historical influence of Scandinavia. It is said that Geordie is the accent and dialect closest to the original form of Anglo-Saxon once spoken throughout the country, probably because the north-east was one of the first areas to be settled by the invading Angles and Saxons, and has been less subject to influence from Latin and Norman French because of its geographical location than more southerly regions of England. For example, the Geordie pronunciation of words such as house ('hoose) and old ('aad') are much closer to their original Anglo-Saxon pronunciation.

Whatever the origins of the word, there is no doubt that Geordie is one of the most distinctive and well-known accents and dialects in the British Isles. Geordie cuisine is becoming increasingly multicultural, but is famed for its traditional broths and pies, and for Singin' Hinnies, large hot cakes cooked on a griddle. Famous Geordies include such diverse personalities as Rowan Atkinson, The Venerable Bede, Jack and Bobby Charlton, Catherine Cookson, Jackie Milburn, George Stephenson and Sting.

Geordie – English

Aa

A Have

A On

Aa I, me

Aa warnd I suppose

Aa'd I had, would

Aa'll I will

Aa'm I am

Aa've I have

Aa, ta To owe

Aabut   Almost

Aad   Old

Aad fashint   Old-fashioned

Aad gadgie   Old man

Aad man, tha   My father

Aad wife   Old woman

Aaful   Awful

Aakwaad   Awkward

Aal   All

Aal reet   All right, ok

Aalwis   Always

Aan   And

Aan   Own

Aanly   Only

Abacka beyont   Far away

Abbut...   Yes, but...

Ableeze   On fire

Aboot   About

Ae   One

Afeard   Afraid

Afore   Before

Agyen   Again

Ahad   Control, a hold of

Ahad   Hold

Ahind, ahint   Behind

Alang   Along

A'len   Alone

Amain   Without restraint
Amang   Among
Amany   Several
Amoont   Amount
An all   Also
Anutha   Another
Anyhoo   Anyhow
Argie, ta   To argue
Arly   Early
Arrain   Rain
Arroar, ta   To roar
Aside of   Next to
Assay   I say
Ate   Eight
Atwix   Between
Ax, ta   To ask
Aye   Yes
Ayont   Behind

Bb

Baad   Sick, ill
Baal   Ball, football
Baal, ta   To cry, shout
Babby   Baby
Back gannin'   Getting worse
Back ower, ta   To return
Back side   Back of a building

Backend   Autumn
Bad-weather Geordie   Cockle seller
Badly liked   Disliked
Badly off   Poor
Baff Week   Miners used to be paid once a fortnight. Baff Week was the second week
Bagie   Belly
Bairn   Child, young teenager
Baist, ta   To beat
Bait   Snack, food
Bait box, can, poke   Something to carry food to work
Bang, ta   To strike violently; to excel
Bank   Steep road or incline
Banky   With many banks or gradients
Bannock   Thick cake of oat, barley or pease meal usually unleavened
Banty   Bantam
Bap   Flat circular bread roll
Bargie   Claim
Bark   Bad cough
Barley, ta   To claim
Barney   Fight, argument
Barry, ta   To bury
Bash, ta   To hit with violence
Basin crop   Hair of head cut straight round a basin
Baste, ta   To thrash
Bat   Blow

Batter, on the   Drinking session

Battered   Tired

Beak   Nose

Beastie   Small animal

Beck   Small stream

Bed-goon   Overall, or any loose garment worn by women

Beggar   Person, fellow

Begox   By God

Behint   Behind (**ahint** is more common)

Belaa   Below

Bellyflapper   Bellyflop (while diving)

Bellytimmer   Food

Berrer-end   Majority

Bested   Beaten

Bet   Bruised by heavy walking

Beuk   A book

Beyut, ta   To boot; something additional paid in a case of barter

Bid, ta   To invite or command

Bide   Wait, stay

Biggin   Building

Bile   Boil

Billy   Companion

Bin   Been

Binno   By this time, by now

Birkie   Smart fellow

Bit   Girlfriend

Bitch, ta   To spoil some work

Biv   By (in front of a vowel)

Blaa   Breath

Blaa oot   Drinking bout

Blaa, ta   To blow

Blabb, ta   To talk loosely

Black Damp   Carbon dioxide in a high concentration underground (lethal if inhaled)

Black diamonds   Coal

Black Pudden   Food made of blood, suet and herbs stuffed into pig's or sheep's intestines

Blackey   Blackbird

Blain, ta   To cry, whimper

Blash   A weak drink

Blate   Awkward, shy

Blather skite   One who talks aimlessly

Blather, ta   To talk nonsense

Bleb   Blister

Bleezer   Metal sheet put in front of fire to get it going

Bliddy, blimin'   Bloody

Blithe   Happy

Blogged   Blocked

Bobbly groond   Bumpy pitch (football)

Body   Person

Bogey   Small cart, often made from a wooden

box on pram wheels

Bogeyman   Hardened nose mucus

Boiley   Milk and bread boiled

Bone, ta   To interrogate

Bonny lad   Handsome man

Bonny, bonny   Good looking, pretty

Bonny lass   Pretty girl

Boody   Broken china (used in children's games)

Bool   Bowl

Bool, ta   To walk

Boolin'   Bowling

Boont   Bound

Booze   Alcohol

Bord   Bird

Born   Burn or large stream

Born, ta   To burn

Borst   Burst

Bowk, ta   To burp, belch

Bowld   Bold

Brahma   Excellent, perfect

Bran' new   Brand new

Brass   Money

Bray, ta   To hit

Brazen   Impudent, shameless

Breed   Bread

Breeks   Trousers

Brewster   Brewer

Brock   Badger
Brockle   Uncertain, fragile, precarious
Broon   Brown (colour)
Broon   Newcastle Brown Ale
Browt   Brought
Bubble, ta   To cry
Bubbly jock   Turkey cock
Bugger   Rough term of affection
Bullets   Sweets
Bully   Brother, comrade
Bummler   Bee
Bummler box   Small house
Buraa…   But I…
Burroo, on the   Unemployed
Buss   Kiss
But and ben   Outside and inside
Buzzem   Broom made of twigs
Byeut   Boot

Cc

Caa oot   Call out
Caa, ta   To call
Caall, ta   To call
Cadge, ta   To beg
Cadger   Beggar
Cakhouse   Toilet
Cakky   Crap, animal or human waste

Callants   Young men, boasters

Caller   Fresh

Candyman   Bailiff; man who serves notice of ejectment; term of abuse or contempt

Canny   Careful with money

Canny   Kindly, good, gentle

Canny few   Large number

Canny toon   Newcastle has long been known to its inhabitants by this description

Canty   Pleasant, lively

Cap, ta   To surpass, complete, tap

Carlings   Choice grey peas, steeped in water for 12–15 hours, until they are soaked. They are then laid on a sieve in the open air so that their outsides may dry. When swelled to a considerable size, and about to sprout, they are put into a pot over a slow fire, and stirred continuously. They will then crack (or bristle): when they begin to burn, they are ready to eat

Cas   Because

Causey   Causeway

Cavil   Draw or lottery to decide work areas in a mine

Chaak   Chalk

Champion   Excellent

Chare   Narrow lane

Cheor   Popular greeting

Cheors   Thank you

Chep Chap
Chicken cre Chicken coop
Chiel Friend
Childer Children
Chimley Chimney
Chimley-neuk Chimney corner
Chine Chain
Chink Money
Chitter-chatter Idle prattle
Choke-damp Also called after-damp, the result of an explosion of fire-damp down the mine
Choller Double chin
Chorch Church
Chow, chew Chewing tobacco
Chow, ta To chew
Chowk, ta To choke
Chuck Bread
Chuck, ta To toss
Chukky Willy
Chunter, ta To grumble
Claa Claw
Clabber Clothes
Claes Clothes
Clag, ta To stick
Claggum Toffee made with treacle
Claggy Sticky
Clammin', Clemmin' Hungry or thirsty

Clarts   Mud, clods of wet earth

Clarty   Dirty, muddy

Clarty, Blash tea   Weak tea

Clash, ta   To slam, close violently

Clatter   Noise

Claver   Gossip

Cleg   Gadfly

Click   Tear, rip in cloth

Click, ta   To snatch

Clip, ta   To strike

Clivvor   Clever, healthy

Clobber   Clothes

Clocker   Sitting hen

Clog   Shoe with a wooden sole

Cloot   Cloth or rag

Clootie baal   Ball made with rags and used by children as a football

Clootie puddin'   Sweet or savoury pudding boiled in a clean cloth

Close   Small enclosure or narrow street

Clot   Stupid fellow

Clout, ta   To strike

Clouts   Clothes

Co-ist   Coast, seaside

Cob   Loaf of bread

Cock-eyed   Squint eyed

Cocked   Drunk

Cockle   Spit

Cocktail   Warm ale with ginger

Cod, ta   To lie, ta pretend

Codger   *see* **Cadger**

Coffin kist   Hearse

Coggly   Unsteady

Coin oot o' the way   Turn aside

Cole   Coal

Colley   Lamplighter

Come and gan   Good store of things

Comin-on   It's raining

Compisision   Composition, school exercise

Conk   Nose

Consart   Concert

Contraband   Cigarettes, pipe, matches or lighter
used for smoking (miners' slang)

Coo   Cow

Coonsil   Local authority

Coonsil hoose   Council house

Copple your creels   Somersault

Copple, ta   To turn over

Corker   Smart reply

Corly   Curly

Corporation   Stomach

Cotterils   Money

Cowld   Cold

Cowp, ta   To upset

Cowt Colt

Coyn, ta To turn

Craa Rook

Craa Crow (bird)

Craa, craw Throat

Crabby Bad-tempered

Crack Gossip

Cracker Fool

Cracket Low stool

Cranky An archaic term for miners

Cree Small hut or pen

Creel Wickerwork basket, carried on the back, used to take hay to sheep in bad weather

Creeps Dislike, horror of

Crikee's Bloody Hell

Croak, ta To die

Croft Small enclosure

Crood Crowd

Croon Crown

Crop, ta To cut hair

Crowdy Oatmeal and boiling water stirred together

Crut Underground incline

Cuddint Could not

Cuddle Embrace

Cuddy Donkey, pony, horse

Cuddy Stupid

Cuddy's legs   Herrings

Cull   Stupid fellow

Cundy   Sewer

Cushat   Ringdove

Cushy   Easy, not difficult

Cutty   Short

Cutty-gun   Short pipe (for tobacco)

Cuty breed   Un-cut loaf of bread

Cyuk   Cook

Dd

Da   Father

Dab   Skilful

Dad   Blow

Daft   Silly

Dafty   Fool

Dagger money   Custom peculiar to Newcastle; this is a gold coin paid to the assize judges when they came from Carlisle. The road was considered so dangerous that the money was paid to provide an armed escort. The money is still paid today

Dain't   Don't

Dang, ta   To strike violently

Darg   Day's work

Darn   Dark

Darn crook   Crooked and dark street

Dash   Shandy

Datal man Man employed by the day

Datalling Odd jobbing

Dee Do

Deed Dead, died

Deed an' gyen Dead and gone

Deed-hoose Mortuary

Deef Deaf

Deein' a bunk Running away

Dell Devil

Demean, ta To lower oneself

Dene Valley through which a burn flows

Deppity Deputy, a man in charge of a section of a mine

Dickies Head lice

Dicky-bord Small bird, always used as a term of endearment

Dike Hedge and/or ditch

Ding, ta To strike

Dinna hev ta Unnecessary

Dinna, dinnet, divvent Do not

Dint, ta To remove part of the mine floor which has lifted

Dirty Wet weather

Disn't Does not

Div Do (before a vowel)

Divart, ta To amuse

Divvint Don't

Dodd, tad Fox

Dog-loup Narrow strip of ground between two houses only wide enough for a dog to pass

Dollup Large piece (of)

Donsie Unlucky

Dook Bath

Dook, ta To duck

Doon Down

Doon-bye Down there, by

Dore, ta To dare

Dorsn't Dare not

Dorty Dirty

Dorty aad tart Dirty old woman

Dother, ta To shake

Dothery Shaky

Dotten aboot Hanging around, sprawling on

Dottle Unburned tobacco left in a pipe after it has been smoked

Dour Sour-looking

Dowie Depressed

Dowtor Daughter

Dozzle Unburned tobacco left in a pipe after it has been smoked

Draa i' pitcher Draw a picture

Draa, ta To draw

Draas Knickers

Drap Drop

Dreed, ta   To dread

Drift   Place driven to reach coal

Drift   Sloping roadway used to access lower or higher areas of the mine

Droond, ta   To drown

Drooned-oot   Flooded mine

Droothy   Thirsty

Dry-dike   Stone wall built without lime

Duccot   Dovecot

Ducks   Faggots (meat balls)

Duds   Miner's working clothes. Sometimes a derisory term for smart clothes

Duff   Coal dust

Duff   Cleugh; the head of a small vale where it is narrowed by opposite craigs

Dump, dumpa   Cigarette butt

Dumplin'   Suet pudding

Dunch, ta   To crash, to knock against

Dunt, ta   To strike on the backside

Dut   Bowler hat

Ee

Ee   Expression of delight

Ee   Eye

Ee   He

Ee   You

Eesell   Himself

Else   Already

Elwis   Always

Ettle, ta   To intend

Ff

Faal   Fall

Faal doon   Fall down

Faal, ta   To fall

Faallen wrang   Become pregnant

Fad   Hobby or whimsical fancy

Fadge   Small flat loaf, generally made from the dough left over after a baking; cottage loaf

Fadge, ta   To eat together

Faff, ta   To mess about

Faggit   Term of contempt

Fair-beat   Exhausted, worn out

Fairin'   Present bought at a fair or from a travelling hawker

Faithor, fether   Father

Fall, in the   In the autumn

Fancy bit   Married man's girlfriend

Far-ower   Much too

Far-ower clivvor   Very cunning and/or clever

Fard   Favoured

Fash   Trouble

Fashion, ta   To resemble

Faws, faas   Gypsy, tinker

Fell   Hill

Femmer   Weak, frail

Femmer   Crumbly

Fenkle   Bend or corner

Fernietickles   Freckles

Fettle   Good condition

Fettle, ta   To repair, to put in order

Feul   Fool

Few   Small number

Fey   State of a person who was supposed to be dying but who would get up and talk with his friends, as if nothing ailed him

Finnie haddie   Finnan haddock (cured with smoke, originally from the village of Findon in Scotland)

Fire damp   Mixture of methane gas and air underground; most dangerous when it reaches 5–15 per cent as then an explosion can occur

Fit as a lop   Fit as a flea

Flaff, ta   To fly about

Flag   Flat sandstones used as roofing tiles

Flaid   Frightened

Flam   Lie, untruth

Flap   Trouser fly

Flapjack   Small cake of flour fried in grease

Flee   Fly

Fling, ta   To throw

Flit, ta   To move from one house to another

Flummix, ta   To surprise
Fly   Crafty
Fly-by-night   An unreliable person
Foist   Damp and sour smell
Foist, ta   To pass something off as genuine
Foisty   Mouldy
Fond   Foolish, silly
Foond   Found
Footrunner   Professional sprinter
For fairs   In earnest, seriously
Forby   In addition to, over and above
Forkytail   Earwig
Fornenst   Against, in front of, opposite
Forrina   Foreigner, or anyone who doesn't speak
   Geordie
Forst   First
Fow   For
Fower   Four
Fowersome   Four persons
Fowt   Fought
Fowty-fower   Forty-four
Foy   Fee, reward
Fratch   Quarrel, disagreement
Fret   Fog on the coast
Fretish   Cold
Frozzin'   Frozen
Full pelt   Full speed

Funnin Joking
Futbaal Football, soccer
Fyece Face

Gg

Ga Gave (in front of a consonant)
Gaak, ta To stare
Gaan Gone
Gaan te pot In a mess
Gab Empty chatter
Gadgie Fellow, bloke, old man employed as a
  watchman
Gaff Theatre or cinema
Gaffer Foreman, boss
Galloway Small horse, originally sourced from
  Galloway, Scotland
Galluses Men's braces
Gammy Lame
Gan arn, ta To go ahead
Gan, ta To go
Gan-on Fuss
Ganner Good goer
Gannin' Going
Gannin' straights Courting couple
Ganny Grandmother
Ganzie Thick woollen jersey, especially worn by
  fishermen

Ganzunder Chamber pot

Garth Guarded or fenced piece of ground

Gate Street or road

Gaumless Silly, ignorant

Gaup, ta To gape or stare

Gav Gave (in front of a vowel)

Ged, ta To get

Gee Stubbornness; taking offence

Geen Given

Geet Great

Geet Really

Geezer Person, queer character

Geordie Dialect spoken on Tyneside

Geordie Native of Tyneside

Geris... Get me...

Get pinched, ta To be arrested

Get shot of, ta To get rid of something or someone

Getten Got

Gew-gaw Mouth organ

Geyen Gone

Geyzened Dried up

Gie, ta To give

Gilif Sudden fright

Gill Place between two steep banks, usually
  wooded

Gimmer Young ewe

Gin If

Ginaan!   Go on! You don't say!

Girdle, gordle   Flat circular iron plate with handle which is used on the open fire for making **Singin' Hinnies**

Girn, ta   To gnash the teeth, to whimper, to pull faces

Giroot!   Get out!

Gissy   Pig

Give-ower!   Who do you think you are kidding? or Stop!

Giz…   Give us…

Gize, ta   To disguise

Gizer   Masquerader

Glair, glaur   Mud, shining dirt, filth

Glaky   Slow witted

Glee-eye   Squint

Gliff   Sudden fright

Glower   Glare

Goaf, Gob   Area left to collapse after coal has been extracted

Gob   Mouth

Gob, ta   To throw something away

Goggley, googley   Staring eyes

Gollar   Growl

Gollup, ta   To gulp one's food

Goniel   Fool, stupid person

Good few   Fair number

Gord   Metal hoop

Gordle-kyek   Cake baked on the girdle

Gorra   Got to

Gowk   Apple core

Gowsty   Gusty

Graan   Grown

Grafflin'   Searching for something with one's hand

Granda   Grandad

Grayne   Clan or family

Greedy hound   One who bolts his food like a dog

Greet   Very

Greet, ta   To cry

Grey hen   Large stoneware bottle, usually containing intoxicating liquor

Gripe   Garden fork

Groop   Drain or ditch

Grosser   Gooseberry

Grumle, ta   To grumble

Grunston   Grindstone

Gud   Good

Guess, ta   To understand

Guessing-story   Conundrum or riddle

Gully   Bread knife

Gutsty   Gluttonous

Gyet   Fool

Gyet   Street (gate)

Gyetsid Gateshead
Gyezend Thirsty

Hh

Haad Hold
Haad on Hold back, hold on
Haak, ta To cough
Haaker Hawker, person who sells fruit and vegetables or fish from a van
Hacka Someone who commits a serious foul in football
Hacky Dirty
Hacky-dorty Very dirty
Hadaway Be gone
Haddin' Holding
Hagger't Beggared
Haggis meat Minced pieces of tripe
Hale Goal at football
Half-cocked Half drunk
Half-nowt Almost nothing
Hammer, ta To strike in a fight, to give a thorough beating to an opponent
Hang-fire Wait
Hanker, ta To hesitate
Hanstorn Work
Hap Overcoat
Hap, ta To cover

Hap-past Half-past

Hard card Poverty

Hardlies Hardly

Harle Heronry

Harr Mist

Harraway! Go away

Harrin' Herring, the favourite (and cheapest)
  Geordie fish

Hasty pudding Oatmeal porridge

Haugh Flat piece of land on a riverside

Hawkie White faced cow

Heather-buzzom Broom made of heather

Heckler Sharp-tongued woman

Hee High

Heed Head

Heer Hair

Help, ta To fill

Hemmel Cattle shed

Heor Here

Hereaway Nearby

Het Exclamation of impatience

Het Hat

Heugh Precipitous hill or cliff

Heuk-nebbed Hook-nosed

Hev, ta To have

Hevna got ta Forbidden, not allowed

Hevvent Have not

Hew, ta   To dig coal

Hewer   Miner who loosens coal with a pick at the coal face

Hinny   Local pronunciation of 'honey'; favourite term of endearment applied usually to women and children

Hint end   Buttocks

Hip, ta   To hop

Hippin-stones   Stepping stones across a stream

Hippins   Nappies

Hippy   Lazy

Hirsel   Stock of sheep belonging to a hill farmer

Hirst   Wood or thicket

Hit   It

Hitch, ta   To hop

Hitty-missy   At random

Hob   Iron pin used in playing quoits

Hoit   Contemptible person

Hoity-toity   Flighty, conceited

Holed through   Breaking through into another mine working

Holey-stone   Stone with a hole in it (natural, not artificial) which was thought to have magic properties

Hoo   How

Hooivvor   However

Hooky   Truancy

Hooky-mat   Mat made from rags and clippings

Hoond   Hound or a low fellow

Hoond-trail   Drag hunt

Hoose   House

Hoose, Wor   Home

Hope   Head of a vale

Hoppings, The   Annual fair held in June in
  Newcastle

Hord   Heard

Hort   Hurt

Hough   Back of the knee

Houlet   Owl

Housin   Capability of holding a lot

How   Salutation

Howay!   Come on!

Howdy   Midwife

Howk, ta   To dig

Howkin'   Punishment, thrashing

Howky   Pitman

Howld, ta   To hold

Hoy, ta   To throw

Hoy-oot   Still sometimes heard at Tyneside
  weddings; the wedding couple are supposed to
  throw coppers to the boys and girls who are calling

Hoyin' oot time   Closing time for a pub

Hoyin' skyul   Gathering of men to play pitch and toss

Huckster   Small tradesman

Huddock   Boat cabin

Huff, ta   To offend

Hule-doo   Figure made of gingerbread or dough and rolled flat; currants are used for eyes

Hump   Temper

Hunk   Large piece (of)

Hunkers, doon on yer   Crouching down

Hut, ta   To heap up

Hutch   Treasure chest

Huzzy   Abbreviated form of housewife

Hyel   Solid coal seam

Hyem   Home

Ii

I'   In (in front of a consonant)

Idle   Immoral

Idle huzzy   Immoral woman

Iggerent   Ignorant

Ilbut   Almost

Ilivven   Eleven

Ill-fard   Ugly-looking

Imp   Naughty child

Impitent   Impudent

In-bye   Within

Inatween   Between

Inby   Inside

Inbye   Away from the pit shaft (underground)

Infomry   Hospital

Ingannin, ta   To go in

Insight   Household goods

Insteed   Instead

Intake   Land taken in and fenced

Intiv   Into

Iroond   Around

Ist   It is

Ist?   Is it?

Itey   Eighty

Iteyite   Eighty eight

Iv'   In (in front of a vowel)

Ivvor   Ever

Jj

Jaa   Jaw

Jaa-breacker   Long word

Jaa, ta   To talk

Jannock   genuine, honest

Jarp, ta   To strike

Jarra   Jarrow (town)

Jeddart Laa   Jedburgh justice, meaning 'hang first, try afterwards'

Jill   Half-pint

Jonty   Diminutive of John

Jort, ta   To jerk

Jowl, ta   To tap the mine roof to see if it is safe

Juggery pokery   Underhand dealing

Jummle, ta   To jumble

Jye   Crooked

Kk

Kaad   Cold

Kang-kang   Haircut which leaves a little fringe at the front

Keek   Soup

Keek, ta   To peep

Keel   Large boat that carried coal on the Tyne

Keep the sump away   Leaving plenty of space for drainage in a wet coal seam

Kelter   Condition, state

Kelter   Money

Ken, ta   To know, to remember

Kep, ta   To catch

Keppy ba'   Handball, ball that is thrown and caught

Kern   End of harvest, celebrated with a kern-supper

Kibble   Bucket used when sinking a new mine shaft

Kid   Child

Kid, Wor   Brother, son

Kiddar   Friend, term of address for children

Kiddy   Son

Kist   Meeting place for miners

Kist o'draas   Chest of drawers

Kist; cist   Box, chest

Kite   Stomach, belly

Kittle, ta   To tickle

Kitty   Prison

Kizzen, ta   To dry up by overcooking

Knaa, ta   To know

Knackered   Tired, worn out

Knakky-kneed   Knock-kneed

Kneddin' kyek   Cake kneaded with lard or butter and baked on a girdle

Knockin' off   Stealing

Knockin-off time   Time to finish work

Knooled   Dispirited

Kye   Cow

Kyek   Cake

Kyel   Soup, broth

Kyevilin' Day   Day when miners would change their work area, usually allocated by lottery or order

Ll

Laa   Low

Lace, ta   To thrash

Lad   Sweetheart

Lads   Group of male friends, not always young people

Laidley   Loathsome

Laith   Unwilling

Lang   Tall, long

Lang last At last

Lang neb Big nose

Lang syne Long since, long ago

Langwidge Language

Larn, ta To teach, to learn

Lashins Plenty

Lass Sweetheart

Lass, Wor My wife

Lasses Group of female friends, not always young people

Lav'rock Skylark

Lavvy Toilet

Lay, ta To stop

Leazes Grass pastures

Lee, ta To lie

Leetnin Dawn

Leev, ta To leave

Leish Lithe, full of youthful vigour

Leister Salmon spear used by poachers

Leuk, ta To look

Lick Small quantity

Lift, ta To steal

Liftin' Moving with life, full of

Liggies Marbles, testicles

Linins Underpants, long-johns

Linn Deep pool at the base of a waterfall; sometimes the waterfall

Lintie   Willow wren

List   Vigour, energy

Load   Large quantity

Loanin, lonnen   Lane or narrow road

Lolly   Tongue

Loopy   Insane, daft

Lop   Flea

Lough   Lake

Lowe   Light

Lowp, ta   To leap, jump

Lowse   End of the shift, knock-off time

Lug   Ear

Lum   Chimney

Lyke   Like, kind of, sort of

Mm

Ma   Mother

Maaky   Maggoty

Mad-het   Very hot

Maimy   Diminutive of Mary

Mair   More

Maisy   Confused

Man   Exclamation used very frequently by
  Geordies

Man   Husband

Man, mun   Must

Marra, ta; marrow, ta   To match, to equal

Marra, marrow   Friend, workmate

Mask, ta   To infuse tea

Mazor   Wonder, an eccentric

Meggie   Diminutive of Margaret

Mell   Wooden mallet

Mesel   Myself

Mevvies   Maybe, perhaps

Mickle, muckle   Much, not little

Mind, ta   To intend, to remember

Minded   Intention

Misdoot, ta   To doubt, to suspect

Mistress   Mrs

Mizzle   Fine rain

Moongin   Moaning, grumbling

Moontin   Mountain

Moot   Meeting

Mooth   Mouth

Mora   Tomorrow

Morda   Murder, not very good

Morn   Tomorrow, morning

Mortalious   Very drunk

Mortle drunk   Blind drunk

Mow   Moment

Muck   Dirt, manure

Muck hut   Heap of manure

Mug   Face, fool

Mugger   Tinker, travelling hawker

Muggles Marbles

Musna Mustn't

Mutha Mother

Myed Made

Myek a song, ta To make a great outcry

Myek, ta To make

Nn

Na No

N'arf Not half

Naa, Nae No

Nag, ta To worry, to criticise

Nakkered Tired, worn out

Nakkers' yard Bone-yard or slaughter-house

Nark, ta To annoy

Narkt Annoyed

Natter, ta To gossip

Neb Nose, beak

Neck Impudence

Nee Haven't any

Nee No

Netty Toilet

Neuk Nook

Newcassell Newcastle (the city)

Nick, ta To undercut a seam of coal

Nigh Near, almost

Nip To pinch

Nit!   Look out behind! (cry of warning)

Nivvor   Never

Nobbut   Only

Noo   Now

Noodle   Yeomanry, cavalry, term of abuse because the local yeomanry were intensely disliked

Nor   Than

Norse   Nurse

Norvis   Nervous

Nowt   Nothing

Numb   Stupid

Nyem   Name

Oo

Oilin' his wig   Drinking heavily

On   Busy with, engaged on

Ooer   Hour

Oot   Out

Oot back   Outside toilet

Oot bye   Outside

Oot bye   Going towards the pit shaft (underground)

Or   Than

Outed   Widely, commonly known

Ov   Of (before a vowel)

Ower   Too

Ower tha moon   Extremely happy

Owt   Anything

Owt mair?   Anything else?
Oxter   Armpit

Pp

Paaky   Conceited

Paan shop   Pawn shop

Pace egg   Hard-boiled painted egg, rolled down the bank in Heaton Park at Easter

Pack   Shepherd's private herd which he grazed in return for his work

Pallatic   Paralytic, very drunk

Pan   Salt pan

Panhaggert, panhagglety   Meal made from potatoes, onions and grated cheese

Pant   Public water fountain

Parkin   Cake made of treacle and oatmeal

Parky   Cold, also particular, fussy about food

Parnickety   Fastidious

Past, ta be   To be distracted

Pay, ta   To thrash

Pease puddin'   Pudding made from split peas and ham. Can be eaten hot or cold

Pelt, ta   To hurry along

Penny gaft   Cheap cinema matinee

Penny lop   Local cinema

Pet   Term of endearment: friend, dear, darling

Peth   Path

Pickle   Small quantity

Pig, piggy   Earthenware hot water bottle

Pigeon cree   Pigeon loft, dovecot

Piggin   Earthenware pitcher

Pike   Pointed hill

Pin   Humour, mood

Pinch, ta   To steal

Pit-yakkor   Term of abuse applied to pitmen

Pitch-an'-toss   Gambling on the result of coins thrown in the air, formerly in general use in the district

Pitmatic   Certain words and expressions peculiar to Geordie miners

Pittle, ta   To urinate

Plash   Heavy rain

Play   Out of work, on sick leave

Ploat, ta   To pluck the feathers from a bird

Plodge, ta   To wade in water with bare feet

Plowd, ta   To wade in mud

Pluff   Plough

Pluff, ta   To spit

Pluffer   Pea-shooter

Poke-puddin'   Pudding boiled in a bag

Poky   Inquisitive

Pollis   Police

Poss-tub   Half a barrel in which the washing was done (obsolete)

Pot-pie   Pie made of beef chopped into pieces surrounded by dough and then boiled in a pot

Pot-shovel   Small shovel for a set-pot

Prog   Half a wooden clothes peg sharpened to a point, used for making mats

Prog, ta   To prod or poke

Proggy mat   Floor covering made out of strips of clean rags poked into sacking with a **prog**

Pump, ta   To break wind

Put ower, ta   To tide over, to survive

Put to reets, ta   To keep orderly

Put, ta   To push, to grow, to throb

Pyel   Pale

Pyet   Head

Qq

Quick   Alert, paying attention

Qweor   Queer, strange

Rr

Raa   Row of houses

Raaf   Timber, odds and ends

Rag, ta   To tease

Rag, ta   To scold

Raim, ta   To talk or call fretfully

Randy   Scolding or quarrelsome woman

Rang   Wrong

Rant   Lively song with chorus

Rap   Bell signal to a machinery operator in a mine. 'Three raps to the winder' indicated that men were about to travel up or down the pit shaft

Rapper   Knocker

Reave, ta   To rob

Redding   Clearing, shifting and tidying up

Rede   Advice

Reed   Red

Reek   Smoke

Reet   Right

Reg'lar randy   Immoral woman

Riding-the-stang   Carrying a man astride a pole; sometimes a punishment for a faithless husband, but among miners it was a sign of triumph

Rig   Ridge

Rive   Tear in a garment

Riving and chewing   Tearing and pulling (coal)

Roondy (coal)   Lumps of coal 4 –8 inches across

Roopy   Hoarse, as with a sore throat

Round the doors   Nearby

Rout, ta   To roar

Rowly-powly   Rolling over and over

Rozzel, ta   To heat over a fire

Rummle, ta   To rumble

Runt   Small ox or cow

Ryte, ta To write
Ryten Writing

Ss

Sackless Useless, simple, stupid
Sad Bad
Samidge Sandwich
Sang Song
Sark Shirt
Scabby Shabby
Scabby Spotty
Scad, ta To scald
Scadd'not Very hot
Scoor, ta To rub clean
Scoot, ta To squirt
Scotch mist Fog on the coast
Scran Bread
Scranchum Gingerbread baked in thin wafers, so
    called because they crackle when eaten; also hard
    skin; crackling on roast pork
Scrat, ta To scratch
Scribe Handwriting
Scrimp, ta To shorten, to act like a miser
Scruffy Dirty
Scruffy aad gadgie Dirty old man
Scrunch, ta To squeeze
Scumfish, ta To choke with smoke

Scunner   Fancy

Scunner, ta   To grimace

Sea coal   Coal washed up on the shore

Sea fret   Fog on the coast

Seek   Sick

Seet   Sight

Sel'   Self

Set-pot   Water boiler set in bricks with a coal fire
  beneath (obsolete)

Setting-stone   Whetstone

Shabby   Applied to health when indifferent

Shag   Covered with long hair

Shake-down   Temporary bed made with a
  mattress and bedclothes on the floor

Sharp   Early, quick

Shaver   Wag

Sheels   North Shields

Shieling   Shelter for sheep

Shift   Shirt

Shift, ta   To move someone or something from
  one place to another

Shiftin'   Removal

Shifty   Unreliable

Shive   Slice

Shoon   Shoes

Shoot, ta   To shout

Short   Abrupt, ill-tempered

Short Shirt

Shot Rid of, clear off

Shu She

Shuggyboat Swing found at fairgrounds

Shy Unwilling, slow

Sic, siccan Such

Side Long, also steep

Siller Silver

Silly Young, innocent, term of affection

Silong Goodbye

Singin' Hinnies Hot girdle cakes, like a large
  scone – best known Geordie food

Sitha! Look!

Sivven Seven

Sivvinty Seventy

Sivvoral Several

Skedaddle, ta To retreat quickly

Skeet Shoe

Skelp, ta To spilt or break off; to strike with the
  open hand particularly on the behind or the cheek

Skemp Short changed

Skep Basket

Skewl School

Skin, ta To beat violently

Skinch Truce (in children's games)

Skint Short of money

Skitters Diarrhoea

Skyet-gob Fish-face

Slack Not busy, not enough

Slack Very small pieces of coal

Slavver, ta To dribble

Sleekit Smooth skinned

Slop Policeman

Slorp, ta To make a noise when eating or drinking with a spoon

Sly-cake Lardy-cake containing currants

Smash Expletive to add emphasis

Smek Hiding place

Smit, ta To infect

Sna'ball Draw Lottery in a working men's club (using numbered balls)

Snaa Snow

Snack, ta To snatch something as a dog does

Snadgee Swede (vegetable)

Snaffle, ta To steal

Snap Snack (usually sandwiches)

Sneck Latch on a door or gate

Snicket Short connection road in a mine

Snitch To tell tales

Snitch Nose

Snob Shoemaker

Snook Beak-like projecting headland

Snotter Mucus from the nose

Snotter-cloot Handkerchief

Sod   Sot

Sonsy   Good looking, pleasant

Spelk   Splinter, slim person

Spice   Gingerbread; also currants mixed with other food

Spice-cake   Currant cake

Spice-kyel   Broth with raisins in

Spittin' image   Likeness

Spuggies' Meeting   Seance; Spiritualists' Meeting

Spuggy   House sparrow

Spuggy   Spirit

Spunk   Courage, spirit

Squint, ta   To peep

St Cuthbert's Beads   Encrinites: fossilised sea animals found on the sands of Holy Island

St Cuthbert's Ducks   Eider ducks

Stangies   Tailors

Stanners   Banks of rivers covered by deposits of stones and gravel

Stannin'   Standing

Steep, ta   To soak, in washing clothes

Stewmer   Tearaway, minor criminal

Stint   Fixed amount of work

Stob   Stump, post

Stoor   Dusty

Stop, ta   To stay, to dwell

Stopple   Tube

Stot, ta   To bounce as a ball

Stotty baaf   Ball for bouncing

Stotty cake   Large flat cake of bread

Stow   Stop

Straa   Straw

Stramp, ta   To trample upon

Strang   Strong

Street   Main road

Stummle, ta   To stumble

Stumor   Stupid

Styfe   Choking smoke

Summik   Something

Sup, ta   To drink

Swally, Swilley   Depression in a mine tunnel
where water may collect

Swanky   Strong young man

Sweir   Unwilling, obstinate

Swig, ta   To drink, to take a heavy draught

Syne   Afterwards

Syun   Soon

Tt

Tab   Cigarette

Tackle, ta   To accost

Taffie   Toffee

Tagareen man   Scrap dealer

Tally, ta   To count, number

Tappy-lappy   Running around aimlessly

Tash   Moustache

Tashin'   On the look-out for girls

Tatie   Potato

Tatie-boggle   Scarecrow

Tatty   Matted

Tawse   Leather strap with end split into five toes
  or fingers; was used in schools for punishment

Tea cloot   Tea towel

Teaser   Problem, an annoyance

Teem, ta   To pour

Telt   Told

Telly-pie   Tell-tale, magpie

Teuk   Took

Tew   Hard and laboured effort

Thaas   You have

Thar'is   That is

Thasel   Yourself

That   So

Thiday   Today

Thimorrow   Tomorrow

Think on, ta   To remember, to consider

Think-shyem, ta   To feel ashamed

Thoosind   One thousand

Thor   Their, they are

Thorty   Thirty

Thowt   Thought

Thrum, ta To purr

Thumpin' Big, hearty

Tice, ta To entice

Tig Sharp blow

Timmer Timber

Tirrah Goodbye

Tommy noddy Puffin; also applies to dwarfs

Toon Town

Toon Army Newcastle United football team & their supporters

Toot 'n oot Keeping a lookout

Tormit Turnip

Tornups Trouser turn ups

Towld Told

Towsher Scruffy person

Trash, ta To wear out with overwork

Tret, tretten Treat, treated

Troozers Trousers

Tundish Funnel

Twank, ta To punish with a strap or cane

Two ooers Two hours

Tyeble Table

Tyek, ta To take

Tyest, ta To taste

Uu

Un One
Unbeknaan Without knowledge of
Uncanny Supernatural
Unco Very
Understrapper Underling
Upby... Up the...
Upcast, ta To bring up as an example
Upstannin Standing
Uptak Understanding
Us Me
Utha Other

Vv

Var nigh Very near
Varra Very
Vast A great deal
Vennel Narrow lane, also a drain
Vine Lead pencil

Ww

Waak, ta To walk
Waal Wall
Waalzender Native of Wallsend
Waar We are
Waard Ward
Waarm Warm

Waasel   Ourself

Wad   Would

Wag   Truant

Wag at the waa   Clock where the weights and
pendulum are visible

Wag, on the   Truant from school

Want, ta   To need

Ward   Word

Wark   Work

Warkyticket   Trouble maker

Warm   Worm

Waster   Useless person

Wat cheor   What cheer (a common Geordie
salutation)

Watta   Water

Waz   Was

Wee, weeny   Little, small

Well-fard   Good looking

Well, of course!   Why aye!

Welt, ta   To lash

Weor   Wear

Wesh, ta   To wash

Weshin   Washing

Weskit   Waistcoat

Whaat?   What?

Whey   Then, well

Whinge, ta   To whine and complain

Whisht Be quiet

White Damp Carbon monoxide in a high concentration underground (lethal if inhaled)

Why aye Yes

Wi' With (before a consonant)

Wid With it

Wife Any staid woman, married or single

Wig Tea-cake

Willicks Whelks (a favourite Geordie shellfish)

Wiv With (before a vowel)

Wiv us With me

Wivoot Without

Wiwih With us

Wor Our

Worm Snake, dragon

Worrit, ta To worry

Wud Would

Yy

Yammer, ta To whine, to complain

Yap Mouth; brat, an impudent child

Yar Your

Yards Measurement of coal face to calculate payments

Yark Heavy blow

Yark, ta To thrash soundly

Ye You

Ye silly billy   Friendly term of abuse

Yel   Ale

Yelhoose   Pub

Yem   Home

Yeor   Year

Yisstidih   Yesterday

Yit   Yet

Yorsel   Yourself

Yous   You (plural)

Yu   You

Yul-doo, yule-babby   Baby figure made of a flat cake of gingerbread or currant cake, and sold to children. The arms are folded across, and two currants are put in for eyes

English – Geordie

Aa

A great deal Vast
About Aboot
Abrupt Short
Accost, to Ta tackle
Act like a miser, to Ta scrimp
Add spirits to tea, to Ta lace
Advice Rede
Afraid Afeard

Afterwards Syne
Again Agyen
Against Fornenst
Alcohol Booze
Ale Yel
Alert, paying attention Quick
All Aal
All right, OK Aal reet
Almost Aabut, ilbut
Almost nothing Half-nowt
Alone A'len
Along Alang
Already Else
Also An all
Always Aalwis, elwis
Among Amang
Amount Amoont
Amuse, to Ta divart
And Aan
Animal or human waste Cakky
Animal, smaller than normal Runt
Annoy, to Ta nark
Annoyance Teaser
Annoyed Narkt
Another Anutha
Anyhow Anyhoo
Anything Owt

Anything else?   Owt mair?

Apple core   Gowk

Argue, to   Ta argie

Armpit   Oxter

Around   Iroond

Arrested, to be   Ta get pinched

Ask, to   Ta ax

At last   Lang-last

At random   Hitty-missy

Autumn   Backend

Autumn   Fall

Away from the pit shaft (underground)   Inbye

Awful   Aaful

Awkward   Aakwaad, blate

Bb

Baby   Babby

Bad   Sad

Bad cough   Bark

Bad-tempered   Crabby, short

Badger   Brock

Bailiff   Candyman

Ball for bouncing   Stotty baaf

Ball made with rags   Clootie baal

Ball, football   Baal

Bantam   Banty

Barley   Bigg

Basket Skep

Basket, wicker Creel

Bath Dook

Be quiet Whisht

Beak Neb

Beat, to Ta baist

Beaten Bested

Because Cas

Bed, temporary Shake-down

Bee Bummler

Been Bin

Before Afore

Beg, to Ta cadge

Beggar Cadger, codger

Beggared Hagger't

Begone Hadaway

Behind Ahind, ahint, ayont, behint

Belch, to Ta bowk

Belly Bagie

Bellyflop (when diving) Bellyflapper

Below Belaa

Bend Fenkle

Between Atwix, inatween

Big Thumpin'

Bird Bord

Blackbird Blackey

Blister Bleb

Blocked   Blogged
Bloke   Gadgie, geezer
Bloody   Bliddy, blimin'
Bloody Hell   Crikee's
Blow   Breath
Blow, to   Ta blaa
Boaster   Callant
Boat, large   Keel
Boil   Bile
Bold   Bowld
Book   Beuk
Boot   Byeut
Boss   Gaffer
Bottle, large stoneware   Grey hen
Bounce as a ball, to   Ta stott
Bound   Boont
Bowl   Bool
Bowler hat   Dut
Bowling   Boolin'
Box or chest   Kist; cist
Braces   Galluses
Brand new   Bran' new
Brat   Yap
Bread   Breed, chuck, scran
Bread knife   Gully
Bread roll   Bap
Bread, uncut loaf of   Cuty breed

Break off, to   Ta skelp

Breath   Blaa

Brewer   Brewster

Bring up as an example, to   Ta upcast

Broken china (used in children's games)   Boody

Broom made of heather   Heather-buzzom

Broom made of twigs   Buzzem

Brother, comrade   Bully

Brother, son   Wor kid

Brought   Browt

Brown (colour)   Broon

Bruised by heavy walking   Bet

Bucket used when sinking a new mine shaft
  Kibble

Building   Biggin

Building, back of a   Back side

Bum   Hint end

Bumpy pitch (football)   Bobbly groond

Burn, to   Ta born

Burp   Bowk

Burst   Borst

Bury, to   Ta barry

Busy with, engaged on   On

But I…   Buraa…

By (in front of a vowel)   Biv

By God   Begox

By this time, by now   Binno

Cc

Cabin, boat's Huddock

Cake Kyek

Cake baked on the girdle Gordle-kyek

Cake fried in fat Flapjack

Cake kneaded with fat, baked on a girdle
  Kneddin' kyek

Cake, treacle and oatmeal Parkin

Cake, currant Spice-cake

Call out, to Ta caa oot

Call, to Ta caa, caall

Capability of holding a lot Housin

**Carbon dioxide in a high concentration
  underground (lethal if inhaled)** Black Damp

**Carbon monoxide in a high concentration
  underground (lethal if inhaled)** White Damp

Careful or mean with money Canny

Cart (child's toy) Bogey

Catch, to Ta kep

Cattle shed Hemmel

Causeway Causey

Chain Chine

Chalk Chaak

Chap Chep

Chest of drawers Kist o'draas

Chew, to Ta chow

Chicken coop Chicken cre

Child Bairn

Children Childer

Chimney Chimley, lum

Chimney corner Chimley-neuk

Choke with smoke, to Ta scumfish

Choke, to Ta chowk

Church Chorch

Cigarette Tab

Cigarette butt Dump, dumpa

Cinema Gaff

Cinema, local Penny lop

Claim, to Ta barley

Claw Claa

Clearing, shifting and tidying up Redding

**Cleugh (head of a small valley where it gets
  narrowed by opposite craigs)** Duff

Cliff Heugh

Clock with visible weights and pendulum
Wag at the waa

Closing time for a pub Hoyin' oot time

Cloth or rag Cloot

Clothes Clabber, claes, clobber, clouts

Clothes peg (half) sharpened Prog

Coal Black diamonds, cole

Coal dust Duff

Coal washed up on the shore Sea coal

Coal, very small pieces Slack

Coast   Co-ist
Cockle seller   Bad-weather Geordie
Cold   Cowld, fretish, kaad, parky
Colt (young horse)   Cowt
Come on!   Howay!
Come, to   Ta cum
Command, to   Ta bid
Companion   Billy
Complain, to   Ta whinge, yammer
Complete, to   Ta cap
Conceited   Paaky
Concert   Consart
Condition, state   Kelter
Confused   Maisy
Connection road (short) in mine   Snicket
Control   Ahad
Cook   Cyuk
Corner   Fenkle
Cough, to   Ta haak
Could not   Cuddint
Council house   Coonsil hoose
Count, number, to   Ta tally
Courage, spirit   Spunk
Courting couple   Straights
Cover, to   Ta hap
Covered with long hair   Shag
Cow   Coo

Cow Kye

Crackling on roast pork Scranchum

Crafty Fly

Crap Cakky

Crash, to Ta dunch

Crooked Jye

Crooked and dark street Darn crook

Crouching down Doon on yer hunkers

Crow (bird) Craa

Crowd Crood

Crown Croon

Crumbly Femmer

Cry, to Ta baal, blain, bubble, greet

Culvert Cully

Curly Corly

Cut hair, to Ta crop

Dd

Damp and sour smell Foist

Dare not Dorsn't

Dare, to Ta dore

Dark Darn

Daughter Dowtor

Dawn Leetnin'

Day's work Darg

Dead and gone Deed an' gyen

Dead, died Deed

Deaf   Deef

Deaf person   Deefee

Deep pool at the base of a waterfall   Linn

Depressed   Dowie

Depression in a mine tunnel   Swally, swilley

Deputy   Deppity

Devil   Dell

Dialect spoken on Tyneside   Geordie

Diarrhoea   Skitters

Dig coal, to   Ta hew

Dig, to   Ta howk

Dirt, manure   Muck

Dirty   Dorty, hacky, scruffy

Dirty old woman   Dorty aad tart

Disagreement   Fratch

Disguise, to   Ta gize

Dish: boiled beef   Pot-pie

Dish: boiled milk and bread   Boiley

Dish: oatmeal , barley or peas   Bannock

Dish: oatmeal and boiling water   Crowdy

Dish: oatmeal porridge   Hasty pudding

Dish: potatoes, onions and grated cheese
   Panhaggert, panhagglety

Dish: pudding boiled in a bag   Poke-puddin'

Dish: split peas flavoured with ham   Pease puddin'

Dish: suet pudding   Dumplin'

Dish: sweet or savoury pudding   Clootie puddin'

Dislike, horror of Creeps
Disliked Badly liked
Dispirited Knooled
Distracted, to be Ta be past
Ditch Groop
Ditch Dike
Do Dee
Do (before a vowel) Div
Do not Dinna, dinnet, divvent
Does not Disn't
Don't Dain't, divvint
Donkey Cuddy
Double chin Choller
Doubt, to Ta misdoot
Dovecot Duccot
Down Doon
Down there, by Doon-bye
Drag hunt Hoond-trail
Dragon Worm
Drain Groop, vennel
Draw a picture Draa i' pitcher
Draw, to Ta draa
Dribble, to Ta slavver
Dried up Geyzened
Drink, to Ta sup, swig
Drinking bout On the batter, blaa oot
Drop Drap

Drown, to   Ta droond

Drunk (in various degrees)
Canny, cocked, half-cocked, oilin' his wig,
   mortalious, mortle drunk, pallatic

Dry up by overcooking, to   Ta kizzen

Duck, to   Ta dook

Dusty   Stoor

Dwarf   Tommy noddy

Dying person   Fey

Ee

Ear   Lug

Early   Arly, sharp

Earwig   Forkytail

Easy, not difficult   Cushy

Eat together, to   Ta fadge

Eccentric person   Mazor

Eider ducks   St Cuthbert's Ducks

Eight   Ate

Eighty   Itey

Eighty-eight   Iteyite

Eleven   Ilivven

Embrace   Cuddle

Empty talk   Gab

Encrinites: fossilised sea animals
St Cuthbert's Beads

End of harvest   Kern

End of the shift, knock-off time   Lowse
Entice, to   Ta tice
Ever   Ivvor
Excel, to   Ta bang
Excellent   Brahma, champion
Exhausted, worn out   Fair-beat
Expletive to add emphasis   Smash
Expression of delight   Ee
Extremely happy   Ower tha moon
Eye   Ee

Ff

Face   Fyece, mug
Faggots (meat balls)   Ducks
Fair number   Good few
Fall   Faal
Fall down   Faal doon
Fall, to   Ta faal
Family   Grayne
Fancy   Scunner
Far away   Abacka beyont
Fart, to   Ta pump
Fastidious   Parnickety
Father   Daa, faithor, fether
Favoured   Fard
Fear, to   Ta dreed
Fee, reward   Foy

Feel around for something, to Ta graffle

Feel ashamed, to Ta think-shyem

Fellow Gadgie

Female Bord (slang)

Fenced or guarded piece of ground Garth

Fight, argument Barney

Fill, to Ta help

Filth Glair, glaur

Find fault, to Ta nag

Fine rain Mizzle

First Forst

Fish-face Skyet-gob

Fit as a flea Fit as a lop

Flat piece of land by a river Haugh

Flea Lop

Flighty Hoity-toity

Flog violently, to Ta skin

Flooded (mine) Drooned-oot

Fly Flee

Fly about, to Ta flaff

Fog, coastal Scotch mist, sea fret

Food Belly-timmer, skran

Fool, stupid person

Clot, cull, dafty, feul, gyet, goniel, mug

Foolish, ignorant, stupid

Cracker, cuddy, daft, fond, gaumless, glaky, loopy,
  numb, stumor

Football, soccer Futbaal

For Fow

Forbidden, not allowed Hevna got ta

Foreigner Forrina

Foreman Gaffer

Fork, garden Gripe

Forty-four Fowty-fower

Fought Fowt

Found Foond

Four Fower

Four persons Fowersome

Fox Dodd

Fragile Brockle

Freckles Fernietickles

Fresh Caller

Friend Chiel, kiddar, marra, marrow

Frightened Flaid

Frozen Frozzin'

Full speed Full pelt

Funnel Tundish

Fuss Gan-on

Fussy about food Parky

Gg

Gadfly Cleg

Gambling game Pitch-an'-toss

Gape or stare, to Ta gaup

Gateshead (town)   Gyetsid

Gathering to play pitch and toss   Hoyin' skyul

Gave (in front of a consonant)   Ga

Gave (in front of a vowel)   Gav

Genuine   Jannock

Get out!   Giroot!

Get rid of something or someone, to   Ta get shot of

Get, to   Ta ged

Getting worse   Back gannin'

Gingerbread   Spice

Gingerbread in thin wafers   Scranchum

Gingerbread man   Hule-doo

Girdle (for cooking)   Gordle

Girdle cakes, hot   Singin' Hinnies

Girlfriend   Bit

Give up the ghost, to   Ta croak

Give us...   Giz...

Give, to   Ta gie

Given   Geen

Glare   Glower

Gluttonous   Gutsty

Go ahead, to   Ta gan arn

Go away!   Harraway!

Go in, to   Ta ingannin

Go on! You don't say!   Ginaan!

Go, to   Ta gan

Goal at football   Hale

Going   Gannin'
Going towards the pit shaft (underground)
   Outbye
Gone   Gaan, geyen
Good   Gud
Good condition   Fettle
Good goer   Ganner
Good health, in   Clivvor
Good looking   Bonny, sonsy, well-fard
Good store of things   Come and gan
Goodbye   Silong, Tirrah
Gooseberry   Grosser
Gossip   Claver, crack
Gossip in an unfriendly way, to   Ta natter
Got   Getten
Got to   Gorra
Grandad   Granda
Grandmother   Ganny
Grass pastures   Leazes
Great   Geet
Grimace, to   Ta scunner
Grindstone   Grunston
Group of female friends   Lasses
Group of male friends   Lads
Grow, to   Ta put
Growl   Gollar
Grown   Graan

Grumble, to   Ta chunter, ta grumle
Gulp one's food, to   Ta gollup
Gusty   Gowsty
Gypsy   Faws, faas

Hh

Hair   Heer
Half-past   Hap-past
Half-pint   Jill
Hand ball   Keppy ba'
Handkerchief   Snotter-cloot
Handsome man   Bonny lad
Handsome woman   Bonny lass
Handwriting   Scribe
Hang him first, try him after   Jeddart Laa
Hanging around   Dotten aboot
Happy   Blithe
Hard and laboured effort   Tew
Hardly   Hardlies
Has   Hez
Hat   Het
Have   A
Have not   Hevvent
Have, to   Ta ha, hev
Haven't any   Nee
**Hawker, person who sells fruit and vegetables
   and fish from a van**   Haaker

He   Ee

Head   Heed, pyet

Head of a valley   Hope

Headland, promontory Snook

Heap up, to   Ta hut

Heard   Hord

Hearse   Coffin kist

Hearty   Thumpin'

Heat over a fire, to   Ta rozzel

Hedge   Dike

Hello there!   How! Wat cheor!

Here   Heor

Heronry   Harle

Herrings   Harrins, Cuddy's legs

Hesitate, to   Ta hanker

Hiding place   Smek

High   Hee

Hill   Fell

Himself   Eesell

Hit, to   Ta bash, ta bray

Hoarse, as with a sore throat   Roopy

Hobby   Fad

Hold   Ahad, haad

Hold back   Haad on

Hold, to   Ta howld

Holding   Haddin'

Home   Wor Hoose, hyem, yem

Honest Jannock

Honey: term of endearment for women and children Hinny

Hook-nosed Heuk-nebbed

Hop on one leg, to Ta hitch

Hop, to Ta hip

Horse Cuddy

Horse, small Galloway

Hospital Infomry

Hot water bottle, earthenware Piggy

Hound Hoond

Hour Ooer

House Hoose

House sparrow Spuggy

House, small Bummler box

Household goods Insight

Housewife Huzzy

How Hoo

However Hooivvor

Humour Pin

Hungry or thirsty Clammin', clemmin'

Hurry along, to Ta pelt

Hurt Hort

Husband Man

Hut or pen, small Cree

Ii

I am   Aa'm
I claim   Bargie
I had, would   Aa'd
I have   Aa've
I say   Assay
I suppose   Aa warnd
I will   Aa'll
I, me   Aa
Idle prattle   Chitter-chatter
If   Gin
Ignorant   Iggerent
Immoral   Idle
Immoral woman   Idle huzzy, reg'lar randy
Impatient exclamation   Het
Impudence   Neck
Impudent   Impitent
Impudent child   Yap
In (in front of a consonant)   Iv'
In a mess   Gaan ta pot
In addition to   Forby
In earnest   For fairs
In front of   Fornenst
Indifferent health   Shabby
Infect, to   Ta smit
Infuse tea, to   Ta mask
Innocent   Silly

Inquisitive   Poky
Inside   Inby
Instead   Insteed
Intend, to   Ta ettle, mind
Intention   Minded
Interrogate, to   Ta bone
Into   Intiv
Invite, to   Ta bid
Is it?   Ist?
It   Hit
It is   Ist
It's raining   Comin-on

Jj

Jarrow (town)   Jarra
Jaw   Jaa
Jerk, to   Ta jort
Jersey, fishermen's thick wool   Ganzie
John (diminutive)   Jonty
Joking   Funnin
Jumble, to   Ta jummle

Kk

Keep orderly, to   Ta put to reets
Keeping a lookout   Toot 'n oot
Kind of   Lyke
Kindly, good, gentle   Canny

82

Kiss Buss

Knee, back of the Hough

Knickers Draas

Knock against, to Ta dunch

Knock-kneed Knakky-kneed

Knocker Rapper

Know, to Ta ken, knaa

Ll

Lake Lough

Lame Gammy

Lamplighter Colley

Land taken in and fenced Intake

Lane or narrow road Loanin, lonnen

Language Langwidge

Lardy-cake containing currants Sly-cake

Large flat loaf Stotty cake

Large number Canny few

Large piece (of) Dollup, hunk

Large quantity Load

Lash, to Ta welt

Latch on a door or gate Sneck

Lazy Hippy

Lead pencil Vine

Leap or jump, to Ta lowp

Learn or teach, to Ta larn

Leather strap with split end Tawse

Leave, to   Ta leev

Lice, head   Dickies

Lie, to   Ta cod, ta lee

Lie, untruth   Flam

Light   Lowe

Like   Lyke

Likeness   Spit an' image

Lithe, full of youthful vigour   Leish

Little, small   Wee, weeny

Lively   Canty

Lively song with chorus   Rant

Loaf   Cob

Loaf, cottage   Fadge

Loathsome   Laidley

Local authority   Coonsil

Long   Lang, side

Long since, long ago   Lang syne

Long word   Jaa-breaker

Look out behind! (warning)   Nit!

Look!   Sitha!

Look, to   Ta leuk

Low   Laa

Low stool   Cracket

Lower oneself, to   Ta demean

Lumps of coal   Roondy (coal)

Mm

Made   Myed

Maggoty   Maaky

Magpie (bird)   Telly-pie

Main road   Street

Majority   Berrer-end

Make a great outcry, to   Ta myek a song

Make a noise when eating or drinking with a spoon, to   Ta slorp

Make, to   Ta myek

Man employed by the day   Datal man

Manure, heap of   Muck hut

Marbles   Allies, liggies, muggles

Margaret (diminutive)   Meggie

Married man's girlfriend   Fancy bit

Mary (diminutive)   Maimy

Match or equal, to   Ta marra, marrow

Matted   Tatty

Maybe   Mevvies

Me   Us

Meeting   Moot

Meeting place for miners   Kist

Mess about, to   Ta faff

Metal hoop   Gord

Metal sheet put in front of fire to get it going   Bleezer

Methane gas and air mixed underground
Fire damp
Midwife   Howdy
Miner   Howky
Mist   Harr
Moaning, grumbling   Moongin
Moment   Mow
Money   Brass, chink, cotterils, kelter
More   Mair
Morning   Morn
Mortuary   Deed-hoose
Mother   Ma, Mutha
Mouldy   Foisty
Mountain   Moontin
Moustache   Tash
Mouth   Gob, mooth, yap
Mouth organ   Gew-gaw
Move from one house to another, to   Ta flit
**Move someone or something from one place to
    another, to**   Ta shift
Moving with life, full of   Liftin'
Mrs   Mistress
Much too   Far-ower
Much, not little   Mickle, muckle
Mucus from the nose   Bogeyman, snotter
Mud, clods of wet earth   Clarts
Muddy   Clarty

Murder,   Morda
Must   Man, mun
Mustn't   Musna
My father   Aad man, tha
My wife   Wor lass
Myself   Mesel

Nn

Name   Nyem
Nappies   Hippins
Narrow lane   Chare, vennel
Narrow street   Close
Narrow strip of ground between two houses
   Dog-loup
Native of Tyneside   Geordie
Native of Wallsend   Waalzender
Naughty child   Imp
Near, almost   Nigh
Nearby   Hereaway, round the doors
Need, to   Ta want
Nervous   Norvis
Never   Nivvor
Newcastle (the city)   Newcassell, Canny toon
Newcastle Brown Ale   Broon
Newcastle United football team & their supporters
   Toon Army
Next to   Aside of

No Naa, nae, nee
Noise Clatter
Nook Neuk
North Shields Sheels
Nose Beak, conk, neb, snitch
Not busy Slack
Not enough Slack
Not half N'arf
Not very good Morda
Notch Nick
Nothing Nowt
Now Noo
Number, small Few
Nurse Norse

Oo

Obstinate Sweir
Odd jobbing Datalling
Of (before a vowel) Ov
Offend, to Ta huff
Old man Aad gadgie
Old woman Aad wife
Old, aged Aad
Old-fashioned Aad-fashint
On A
On fire Ableeze
On sick leave Play

On the look-out for girls   Tashin'

One   Ae, un

One thousand   Thoosind

One who talks aimlessly   Blather skite

Only   Aanly, nobbut

Opposite   Forenenst

Other   Utha

Our   Wor

Out   Oot

Outside   Oot bye

Outside and inside   But and ben

Outside toilet   Oot-back

Over and above   Forby

Overall or any loose garment worn by women
   Bed-goon

Overcoat or extra covering   Hap

Owe, to   Ta aa

Owl   Houlet

Own   Aan

Pp

Pale   Pyel

Parched, thirsty   Gyezend

Particular (in a fussy way)   Parky

Pass something off as genuine, to   Ta foist

Path   Peth

Pawn shop   Paanshop

Pea-shooter   Pluffer
Peep, to   Ta keek, squint
Perfect   Brahma, champion
Perhaps   Mevvies
Person, fellow   Beggar, body
Pig   Gissy
Pigeon loft   Pigeon cree
Pinch, to   Ta nip
Pipe (tobacco), short   Cutty-gun
Pitcher, earthenware   Piggin
Place driven to reach coal   Drift
Player who commits a serious foul in football   Hacka
Pleasant   Bonnie, bonny, sonsy
Plenty   Lashins
Plough   Pluff
Pluck a bird, to   Ta ploat
Pointed hill   Pike
Police   Pollis, slop
Pony   Cuddy
Poor   Badly off
Post (wooden)   Stob
Potato   Tatie
Pour, to   Ta teem
Poverty   Hard card
Precarious   Brockle
Pregnant, to become   Faallen wrang

Present bought at a fair or from a hawker   Fairin'
Pretend, to   Ta cod
Pretty   Bonny, sonsy
Pretty girl   Bonny lass
Prison   Kitty
Problem   Teaser
Prod or poke, to   Ta prog
Pub   Yelhoose
Puffin (bird)   Tommy noddy
Pull faces, to   Ta girn
Punish with a strap or cane, to   Ta twank
Punishment   Howkin'
Purr, to   Ta thrum
Push, to   Ta put
Putting on airs   Hoity-toity

Qq

Quantity, small   Lick, pickle
Quarrel   Fratch
Queer character   Geezer
Queer, strange   Qweor

Rr

Rag mat   Hooky-mat, proggy mat
Rain   Arrain
Rain, heavy   Plash
Really   Geet

Red (colour)   Reed

Remember, to   Ta ken, think on

Removal   Shiftin'

Remove part of the mine floor which has lifted, to
   Ta dint

Repair or put in order, to   Ta fettle

Resemble, to   Ta fashion

Retreat quickly, to   Ta skedaddle

Return, to   Ta back ower

Rid of, clear of   Shot

Riddle   Guessing-story

Ridge   Rig

Right   Reet

Ringdove   Cushat

River bank   Stanner

Roar, to   Ta arroar, rout

Rob, to   Ta reave

Rolling over and over   Rowly-powly

Rook (bird)   Craa

Row of houses   Raa

Rub clean, to   Ta scoor

Rumble, to   Ta rummle

Runner, professional   Footrunner

Running around aimlessly   Tappy-lappy

Running away   Deein' a bunk

Salmon spear, poacher's   Leister

Salt pan   Pan

Sandstone roofing tiles   Flag

Sandwich   Samidge

Scald, to   Ta scad

Scarecrow   Tatie-boggle

School   Skyul

School essay   Compisision

Scold, to   Ta rag

Scrap dealer   Tagareen man

Scratch, to   Ta scrat

Dirty old man   Dorty aad gadgie

Scruffy person   Towsher

Seance; Spiritualists' Meeting

Spuggies' Meeting

Seaside   Co-ist

Self   Sel'

Seriously   For fairs

Seven   Sivven

Seventy   Sivvinty

Several   Amany, sivvoral

Sewer   Cundy

Shabby   Scabby

Shake, to   Ta dother

Shaky   Dothery

Shameless   Brazen

Shandy (beer and lemonade drink)   Dash

She   Shu
Sheep shelter   Shieling
Sheep, young   Gimmer
Shelter   Bield
Shirt   Sark, shift, short
Shoe   Skeet
Shoemaker   Snob
Shoes   Shoon
Short   Cutty
Short changed   Skemp
Short of money   Skint
Shout, to   Ta baal
Shout, to   Ta shoot
Shush!   Wisht!
Shy   Blate
Sick, ill   Baad, seek
Sight   Seet
Silver   Siller
Sitting hen   Clocker
Skilful   Dab
Skylark   Lav'rock
Slam, close violently, to   Ta clash
Slaughter-house   Nakkers' yard
Slice   Shive
Slim person   Spelk
Slow   Shy
Small animal   Beastie

Small bird (affectionate) Dicky-bord

Small enclosure Croft, close

Smart clothes (derisive) Duds

Smart fellow Birkie

Smart reply Corker

Smoke Reek

Smoke, choking Styfe

Smoking, items for Contraband

Smooth skinned Sleekit

Snack (usually sandwiches) Bait, snap

Snake Worm

Snatch, to Ta click, snack

Snow Snaa

So That

Soak, to Ta steep

Somersault, turn a Copple your creels

Something Summik

Something additional paid in a barter Ta beyut

Something to carry food to work Bait box, can, poke

Son Kiddy

Song Sang

Soon Syun

Sort of Lyke

Sot Sod

Soup or broth with raisins in Spice-kyel

Soup, broth Keek, kyel

Sour-looking   Dour
Spill, to   Ta skelp
Spirit   Spuggy
Spit   Cockle
Spit, to   Ta pluff
Splinter of wood   Spelk
Spoil some work, to   Ta bitch
Spotty   Scabby
Sprawling on   Dotten aboot
Squeeze, to   Ta scrunch
Squint eyed   Cock-eyed, glee-eyed
Squirt, to   Ta scoot
Standing   Stannin', upstannin'
Stare, to   Ta gaak
Staring eyes   Goggley, googley
Stay   Bide a bit
Stay, to   Ta stop
Steal, to   Ta lift, pinch, snaffle
Stealing   Knockin' off
Steep   Side
Steep road or incline   Bank
Stepping stones across a stream   Hippin-stones
Stick, to   Ta clag
Sticky   Claggy
Sticky toffee   Claggy taffie
Stomach   Corporation, kite
Stone wall built without lime   Dry-dike

Stone with a natural hole in it Holey-stone
Stop Stow
Stop it! Give-ower!
Stop, to Ta lay
Straw Straa
Stream Beck, born
Street or road Gate, gyet
Strike, to
Ta bang, clip, clout, dang, ding, dunt, hammer,
  jarp, skelp
Strong Strang
Strong young man Swanky
Stubborness Gee
Stumble, to Ta stummle
Stump Stob
Stupid Sackless
Stupid person, fool
Clot, cull, dafty, feul, gyet, goniel, mug
Stupid, foolish, ignorant Cracker, cuddy, daft,
  fond, gaumless, glaky, loopy, numb, stumor
Such Sic, siccan
Sudden fright Gliff
Supernatural Uncanny
Surpass, to Ta cap
Surprise, to Ta flummix
Survive, to Ta put ower
Suspect, to Ta misdoot

Swede (vegetable)   Snadgee
Sweetheart (female)   Lass
Sweetheart (male)   Lad
Sweets   Bullets
Swing, once common at fairs, with seats across
  like a boat   Shuggyboat

Tt

Table   Tyeble
Tailors   Stangies
Take, to   Ta tyek
Taking offence   Gee
Talk loosely, to   Ta blabb
Talk nonsense, to   Ta blather
Talk or call fretfully, to   Ta raim
Tall   Lang
Tap the mine roof to see if it is safe, to   Ta jowl
Taste, to   Ta tyest
Tea towel   Tea cloot
Tea, weak   Clarty tea, blash tea
Tea-cake   Wig
Teach or learn, to   Ta larn
Tear in cloth or garment   Click, rive
Tearaway, minor criminal   Stewmer
Tearing and pulling (coal)   Riving and chewing
Tease, to   Ta rag
Teenager, young   Kid

Tell tales, to Ta snitch
Tell-tale Telly-pie
Temper Hump
Term of abuse
Candyman, faggit, greedy hoond, hoit, noodle, waster
Term of abuse (miners) Pit-yakkor
Term of address for children Kiddar
Term of affection (rough) Bugger
Term of endearment Hinny, pet, silly billy
Testicles (marbles) Liggies
Than Nor, or
Thank you Cheors
That is Thar'is
Theatre Gaff
Their Thor
Then, well Whey
They are Thor
Thicket Hirst
Thirsty Clammin', clemmin', droothy
Thirty Thorty
Thought Thowt
Thrash, to Ta baste, lace, pay, yark
Thrashing Howkin'
Throat Craa, craw
Throb, to Ta put
Throw out! Hoy-oot!

Throw something away, to   Ta gob
Throw, to   Ta fling, ta hoy
Tickle, to   Ta kittle
Tide over, to   Ta put ower
Timber   Timmer
Timber, odds and ends   Raaf
Time to finish work   Knockin-off time
Tinker, travelling salesman   Faws, faas, mugger
Tired   Battered, knackered, nakkered
To   Ta
To (before a vowel)   Tiv
Tobacco, chewing   Chow, chew
Today   Thiday
Toffee made with treacle   Claggum
Toilet   Cakhouse
Toilet   Lavvy, netty
Told   Telt, towld
Tomorrow   Mora, thimorrow
Tongue   Lolly
Too   Ower
Took   Teuk
Toss, to   Ta chuck
Town   Toon
Tradesman, small   Huckster
Trample upon, to   Ta stramp
Treasure chest   Hutch
Treated   Tret, tretten

Tripe, minced pieces of   Haggis meat
Trouble   Fash
Trouble maker   Warkyticket
Trouser fly   Flap
Trouser turn ups   Tornups
Trousers   Breeks, troozers
Truancy   Hooky
Truant from school   Wag, on the
Truce (in children's games)   Skinch
Truncated hill   Dodd
Tube   Stopple
Turkey cock   Bubbly jock
Turn aside   Coin oot o' the way
Turn over, to   Ta copple
Turn, to   Ta coyn
Turnip   Tormit
Two hours   Two ooers

Uu

Ugly-looking   Ill-fard
Unburned tobacco left in a pipe after it has been smoked   Dozzle, dottle
Uncertain   Brockle
Undercut a seam of coal, to   Ta nick
Underground incline   Crut
Underhand dealing   Juggery pokery
Underling   Understrapper

Underpants, long-johns   Linins
Understand, to   Ta guess
Understanding   Uptak
Unemployed   On the burroo, play
Unlucky   Donsie
Unnecessary   Dinna hev ta
Unreliable   Shifty
Unsteady   Coggly
Unwilling   Laith, shy, sweir
Unwilling pupil   Diller
Up the...   Upby...
Upset, to   Ta cowp
Urinate, to   Ta pittle

Vv

Valley through which a stream flows   Dene
Very   Greet, unco, varra
Very cunning, clever   Far-ower clivvor
Very dirty   Hacky-dorty
Very hot   Mad-het, scadd'not
Very near   Var nigh
Vigour, energy   List

Ww

Wade in mud, to   Ta plowd
Wade in water with bare feet, to   Ta plodge
Wag   Shaver

Waistcoat   Weskit

Wait   Bide, hang-fire

Walk, to   Ta bool, ta waak

Wall   Waal

Ward   Waard

Warm   Waarm

Warm ale with ginger   Cocktail

Was   Waz

Wash, to   Ta wesh

Washing   Weshin'

Watchman   Gadgie

Water   Watta

Water fountain, public   Pant

We are   Waar

Weak, frail   Femmer

Weak drink   Blash

Wear   Weor

Wear out with overwork, to   Ta trash

Well, of course!   Why aye!

Wet weather   Dirty

What?   Whaat?

Whelks   Willicks

Whetstone   Setting-stone

Whimper, to   Ta blain

Whine and complain, to   Ta whinge, ta yammer

White faced cow   Hawkie

Who do you think you are kidding?   Give-ower!

Who finds keeps   Findy-keepy
Widely, commonly known   Outed
Willow wren   Lintie
Willy   Chukky
With (before a consonant)   Wi'
With (before a vowel)   Wiv
With it   Wid
With many banks or gradients   Banky
With me   Wiv us
With us   Wiwih
Within   In-bye
Without   Wivoot
Without check   Amain
Without knowledge of   Unbeknaan
Woman, scolding and quarrelsome   Randy
Woman, sharp tongued   Heckler
Woman, staid   Wife
Wonder   Mazor
Wood   Hirst
Wooden mallet, mason's   Mell
Word   Ward
Work   Hanstorn, wark
Work, fixed amount of   Stint
Working clothes (miner)   Duds
Workmate   Marra, marrow
Worm   Warm
Worn out   Battered, knackered, nakkered

Worry, to   Ta nag, ta worrit
Would   Wad, wud
Write, to   Ta ryte
Writing   Ryten
Wrong   Rang

Yy

Year   Yeor
Yes   Aye, why aye
Yes, but...   Abbut...
Yesterday   Yisstidih
Yet   Yit
You   Ee, ye, yu
You (plural)   Yous
You have   Thaas
Young   Silly
Young men   Callants
Your   Yar
Yourself   Thasel, yorsel

Wicked Geordie Phrases

Aa

A caad neet, but there's nee snaa
A cold night, but there is no snow

A d'ye at tha ce'ust   A day at the coast, or seaside

A greet click iv her frock
A great tear in her dress

A waak long th' Waal
A walk along Hadrian's Wall

Aa aa nowt   I owe nothing

Aa canna bide yon chap   I really dislike that man

Aa daint knaa   I don't know

Aa daint owe ye owt   I don't owe you anything

Aa divven' knaa, hinny   I don't know, darling

Aa divvent knaa his nyem   I don't know who he is

Aa haad a pittle lyke   I had to urinate

Aa henna tha list to dee'd
I haven't the energy to do it

Aa hev nee tatties   I have no potatoes

Aa hevn't deun a hanstorn tha day
I haven't done any work today

Aa just took a keek iv ta find oot what wis on
I just came in to find out what was happening

Aa lyke ye   I like or love you

Aa naa!   I know!

Aa sarved me time tiv a shoemaker
I was apprenticed to a shoemaker

Aa see it's aall reet; it's puttin'
The plant is not dead; it's putting out buds

Aa syun foond oot   I soon found out

Aa tellt yu   I told you

**Aa teuk tha chance to sit doon on me hunkers to
    leet me pipe**
I took the opportunity to squat down and light my
    pipe

Aa thowt se   I thought so

Aa towld them   I told them

Aa wad a thowt se   I would have thought so

Aa wad be laith ti gan win him
I wouldn't go with him

Aa waddent demean mesel to de sic a thing
I wouldn't stoop so low as to do that

Aa warnd ye think yorsel' clivvor?
I suppose you think yourself clever
Aa wis nigh lossin' me hat   I almost lost my hat
Aa'd a been there mesel
I would have been there myself
Aa'd better gan canny   I had better be careful
Aa'd nowt left   I had nothing left
Aa'll clip yer lug   I will strike your ear
Aa'll de it tha mora   I'll do it tomorrow
Aa'll ettle to be there, noo, if I can
I intend to be there now, if I can
Aa'll gie ye a skelp o' tha lug
I will smack your head
**Aa'll gie ye sic a byestin' as ye nivver got i' yer
  life**
I'm going to give you the worst beating of your
  life
Aa'll give ye i' pound ter beyut
I'll give you an extra pound
Aa'll hammer ye   I'll give you a good hiding
Aa'll howk yer eyes oot   I will poke your eyes
  out
Aa'll just say gud neet   I will just say good night
Aa'll lace ye   I'll give you a good hiding
Aa'll pay yer hide   I'll give you a good hiding
Aa'll skin ye if aa get ahad on ye
If I catch you I will give you a good hiding

Aa'll tackle that job   I'll do that job

Aa'll yark yer hide for ye
I'll give you a good hiding

Aa'm clamming for a drink
I'm dying for a drink

Aa'm cushy iboot it   I am not really bothered

Aa'm gaan oot   I'm going out

Aa'm gaanin' yem   I'm going home

Aa'm gannin' hyem   I'm going home

Aa'm gannin' oot with wor lass tha neet
I am going out with my wife (or girlfriend)
    tonight

Aa'm ower heed i' luv   I am deeply in love

Aa's dreedin' tha worst hinny
I'm expecting the worst, darling

Aa's fit te chowk   I need a drink

Aa's gaan doon-bye   I'm going down there

Aa's iv a horry   I'm in a hurry

Aa's nobbut badly thi day
I am feeling sick today

Aa's sweetin' like a mugger's cuddy
I'm sweating like a tinker's pony

Aa's trashed ti deed   I'm exhausted

Aa've a broakin' hart   I have a broken heart

Aa've a good mind ti clash yer jaa
I feel like hitting you on the chin

Aa've getten a stitch i' me side
I've got a pain in my side
Aa've gorra gaan noo
I've got to go now
Aa've hed a fashous job on't
I've had a troublesome job with it
Aa've prog'd me thoom wiv a needle
I've pricked my thumb with a needle
Aa've tew'dat tha job till aa's paid
I've done my best at this job but I've been defeated
Aal graan up   All grown up
Aal togither like tha folks o' Shields
Tyneside proverb that illustrates the clannishness
    of the people of Shields
Aam gaanin' by mesel   I'm going by myself
Afore ee gaan   Before you go
Are ye aalreet, hinny?
Are you all right, sweetheart / darling?
Are ye cummin' wiwih?
Are you coming with us?
**At ivery yellhoose i' this toon we haad a cocktail
    po**
We had a drink at every pub in town
Ax wor lass   Ask my wife

Bb

Baal yer eyes oot   Cry your eyes out

Bella an' hims tyen on
Bella and he have become an item

Bide heor   Wait here

Blaa tha leet oot   Blow out the light

Bliddy / blimin' hek!   Bloody hell!

Bool doon tha road   Walk down the road

Bool tha baal   Roll the ball

Boont ta de it   Bound to do it

Bran new coat, but aad breeks
New coat, but old trousers

Broons alroond!
Beer for all my friends, please!

Bura daint knaa   But I don't know

Byeut i' tha hintend   Kick in the backside

Cc

Caan yu tyest that, pet?
Can you taste that, darling?

Can aa gan?   Can I go?

Can yu de it fow'u lyke?   Can you do it for us?

Canny aad body   Wise, sneaky old woman

Canny aad bugger/chep   Wise, sneaky old man

Canny good   Very good

Cheer up, hinny, dinna look dowie
Cheer up, darling, at least look happy

Chuck it ower heor   Throw it over here
Clag it on   Stick it on
Come bye!   Get out of the way!
Come thee ways   Come forward
Coyn tha corner   Turn round the bend
Cruck yer hough!   Sit down!

Dd

Dear knaas what aa's gan te dee
I do not know what I am going to do
Dee as yer bid!   Do what you're told!
Deel tyek ye!   The devil take you!
Dinna stramp ower tha clean iloor
Don't trek dirt on my floor
Div aa knaa him?   Do I know him?
Divvint argie!   Don't argue!
Divvint be sih impitent!   Don't be so cheeky!
Divvint be se parky!   Don't be so fussy!
Divvint clash tha door!   Don't slam the door!
Divvint dee that!   Don't do that!
Divvint gan iv tha clarts!   Keep out of the mud!
Divvint shuv!   Don't push!
Divvint snitch on me!   Don't betray me!
Divvint ye baal at me!   Don't you shout at me!
Do yu ken?   Do you know?
Dollup of kyek   Large slice of cake
Dook yer heed   Duck your head

Doon ta tha buff Stripped naked

Draa on i' tab Puff on a cigarette

Ee

Ee aalwis ses that He always says that

Ee clicked it oot o' me hand
He knocked it out of my hand

Ee cum forst He came first

Ee disn't knaa oot He does not know anything

Ee divvent scunner me at all He didn't notice me

Ee droonded hisell He drowned himself

Ee flummix'd him He had the best of the
  argument

Ee gives is tha creeps I really dislike him

Ee glowered at him He glared at him

Ee got a rare raggin' ower tha job
He was severely scolded for his work

Ee got sic a dad as ee'll not forgit
He won't forget that blow in a hurry

Ee hez a good housin' for drink
He can really hold his drink

Ee hez far ower much ti say for hissell
He's far too pushy

Ee hez nee spunk at a' He has no guts

Ee hez nowt He's broke

Ee jawed a heap of blather
He talked a load of nonsense

Ee just raimed away like one oot iv his heed
He raved and shouted like a madman
Ee lives abacka beyont
He lives in a very remote place
Ee lucks, poor body, verra bad
Poor man, he looks very sick
Ee ses what?   He said what?
Ee taaks a reet load
He talks nonsense (a load of rubbish)
Ee thowt he haad, but he hadn't
He thought he had, but he hadn't
Ee wes slow i' tha uptak   He's stupid
Ee wis barkin' his heed off
He was coughing very badly
Ee wis haddin' on for bare life
He was hanging on for dear life
Ee wis quite short wi' me   He was rude to me
Ee wis varry laa doon   He was in very low
   spirits
Ee wis very narkt   He was very annoyed
Ee'll be there tha morn
It/he will still be there tomorrow
Ee'll blabber and taak all neet
He'll not stop talking all night
Ee'll not put-ower tha neet   He's about to die
Ee's a crabby aad chep   He's difficult
Ee's a greet sackless cuddy   He's a fool

Ee's a greet sod   He's a terrible drunkard

Ee's a reet mug   He's a fool

Ee's a stumor   He's difficult

Ee's a workie ticket   He's a trouble maker

Ee's as active as a lintie   He has quick reactions

Ee's canny wiv his coppers
He is careful with his money

Ee's elwis gan moongin' aboot
He's always going around grumbling

Ee's fond as a besom   He's a fool

Ee's getten a gammy leg   He's lame

Ee's getten his hump up   He's in a bad temper

Ee's havin' a wee   He's urinating

Ee's howkin' taties   He's digging up potatoes

Ee's iv a bad fettle   He's in a bad temper

Ee's iv a sad way   He's not well

Ee's just clartin' on   He is messing about

Ee's me marra   He's my friend

Ee's nee greet shakes, onyway
He's not a reliable person

Ee's not bonny-leukin', but he's a ganner
He's not good-looking, but he'll do the job

Ee's on tha batter agyen
He's getting drunk again

Ee's on tha netty   He's in the toilet

Ee's oot on the booze   He's getting drunk

Ee's playin' hooky   He's playing truant from school

Ee's sweir ta pairt win his money
He's unwilling to spend his money

Ee's tyen a scunner at her
He really fancies her

Ee's tyen tha huff   He is offended

Ee's varry shabby thi' day   He's not well today

Eh, what a canny body!
He/she is such a nice person

Ff

Folks dorsent say owt tiv him
He's in a bad temper

Gg

Gan roon' tha corner; it's ower gowsty here
Come round the corner, it's too cold here

Gan yer ann gate   Go your own way

Gannin' doon tha co-ist   Going to the seaside

Gannin' hyem   Going home

Ganning straights   They are courting seriously

Ged oot! Geroot!   Get out!

Ged owa tha waal   Get over the wall

Geet big gob   Great big mouth

Geris a poond aa tatties
Get me a pound of potatoes

Get ahad of it   Take control (implied: you fool)

Get oot, ye clarty faa   Get out, you dirty slut

Get yer blaa   Rest till your breath comes back

Give ower bubblin'!   Stop crying!

Give ower yammerin'!   Stop whining!

Giz a drink, I'm gyezend

Give me a drink, I'm desperate

Giz a pickle mair   Give me a little more

Giz i bit…   Give me a piece of…

Haad on a min't / mow

Please wait, hold on a minute

Haad tha bairn   Hold the baby

Haad yer gob!   Shut up!

Haad yer tung!   Shut up!

Haad yer whisht!   Shut up!

Hadaway seek tha milk   Go and buy some milk

Hadaway!

Stop it, go away; also used to encourage

Hap weel up, it's a caad neet

Wrap yourself up, it's a cold night

Has ann uncanny way aboot her

She can be quite spooky

He teuk the gee   He was very stubborn

He's nee greet shakes, onyway

He's not a reliable person

**Here's thumpin' luck to yon toon, let's hev a
hearty drink upon't**   Cheers

Here's to Newcastle!   Bottoms up!

Hev enny on'ye?

General request when looking for small change for
parking meter, etc.

Hev y'got th'time on'ye?

Can you tell me the time please?

Hev ye got owt?   Have you got anything?

Hev ye haad a dook yit?

Have you had your bath yet?

Hev yu browt it?   Have you brought it?

Hez ee been?   Has he been?

His claes wis liftin' wi' varmin'

His clothes were crawling with lice and fleas

Hoo bin ye tha day?   How are you?

Hoosit gannin' a th'match?

How is the football match progressing?

Hor bedgoon is laelock

Her jacket is lilac in colour

How d'ye get ower toon like?

What is the best way to get to town?

How there, marra?   How are you, my friend?

How ye gannin', kidder?

How are you, my friend?

Howay doon tha chippy (Chinese, Tandoori, etc), pet, ah'm clammin'
Let's go and get something to eat from the take-away restaurant, I am hungry

Howay lads, it's lowse   Time gentlemen

Howay man!   Come along, hurry up

Howay tha Lads! Toon Army!
Up with Newcastle United!

Hoy oot!
Children's cry for groom and guests at weddings to throw them coins for luck

Hoy tha baal   Throw the ball

Hoy-ye!   Hailing a taxi

Ii

Iroond ha'past fower   Around half-past four

It fits him tiv a tee   It fits him perfectly

It waz ee at did it   It was you who did it

It waz greet big   It was huge

It's a bit hissy-missy   It's hit or miss

It's canny het th'd'ye   It is a fine warm day

It's gyen all ta smithereens   It's broken in pieces

It's lone wivoot him   I'm lonely without him

It's me dowtor lyke   She's my daughter

It's narf caad   Isn't it cold

It's nivvor stottin-doon
We rarely have heavy rain!

It's pittling doon   It's raining
It's teeming cats an' dogs   It's raining very hard
It's varra caad oot bye   It's very cold outside

Jj

Just i kid   Just a youngster

Kk

Keep ahaad, gan canny
Take care of yourself, go carefully
Keep yer lang-neb oot o' this!
Mind your own business!

Ll

Lashins o' meat and drink
Plenty of food and drink
Leave him / it a'len   Leave him / it alone
Let's hev a plodge i' tha watter
Let's paddle in the sea
Let's hev a squint at tha papers
Let me read the newspapers
Let's howay doon tha booza   Let's go for a drink
Look ahind yu   Look behind you
Look oot belaa   Look out below
Lowp ower tha waal   Jump over the wall
Luk at tha arse on that!
Look at that woman's bottom!

Mm

Man, aa's clivvor I'm very pleased with myself

Maybies aa wull gan Perhaps I will go

Me aan fireside Home

Me Ant Annie wis aalwis bowkin'

My Aunt Annie was always burping

Me hand's puttin', an' aa's flaid it's gan ti beeld

My hand is aching, and I'm afraid it is going to
  bleed

Mind me on Remind me

Mind ye dinna stop ower lang

Be sure you don't stop too long

Nn

Nice leukin' bord Nice looking woman

Nivvor mind Don't worry

Not reet iv his head He's mad

Nowt but canny

Very well, thank you (in response to 'What fettle
  tha day?')

Oo

Oppen thy gob, hinny, and put out thy lolly

Open your mouth, child, and put out your tongue

Ower heor Over here

Ower tha watter Across the River Tyne

Pp

Play thu wag, ta   To play truant from school
Reed hot!   Red hot!
Roond tha bend   Around the bend
Rozzel yer shins   Warm yourself by the fire

Ss

See that tha door's put to   Shut the door!
See yer drinks off lads   Time, gentlemen, please
Seek ta deed   Sick to death
She bash't me   She hit me
She bashed tha door i' me fyece
She closed the door in my face
She canna cyuk   She can't cook
She hes an uncanny way wiv her
She can be very spooky at times
She set off tha aafulest shrieks
She screamed her head off
She wis gan a waak wiv her lad
She was out walking with her sweetheart
**She's alwes chunteren on, nivvor content wi
   nowt**   She's always complaining and never
   satisfied
She's been oot seekin' aal day
She's been out all day asking for charity
She's gotten tha scunners   She's taken offence
She's i canny lass   She is a nice girl

She's kizzened tha pot
She's burned the food
She's lost her nick
She had lost her reckoning of time
She's nobbut femmer, poor body
She's frail, poor soul
She's on tha batter   She's a prostitute
Short rede is good rede
The best advice is the most concise
Shut yer yap   Shut your mouth
Siccan a fight as we haad, I neer saw iv a' my days
The best fight I've ever seen/ taken part in
Stow that, now!   Stop that at once!
Summicks bornin'   Something is burning

Tt

Tatty heed   Insult to a young woman
Teem oot tha tea   Pour out the tea
That's hit noo...   That's it then...
The aad miser's as scrimpy as can be
The old miser is as mean as can be imagined
The bairns haad been badly tretten
The children had been badly treated
The bairns hez all getten gords ti play wi'
The children were all given hoops to play with
The bairns were blain'n'
The children were crying

The cat's happy; d'ye hear hor thrummin?

The cat's happy; can you hear her purring?

The chimley's been smokin' till aa's fair scumfished

The chimney has smoked so much that I'm choking

The chimley's reekin' badly

The chimney is smoking badly

The hailstones wis stotin' off tha hoose-tops

The hailstones were bouncing off the roofs

The hoose is ablaze   The house is on fire

The hoose is crooded out

The house is very crowded

The lock wants fettlin'   The lock needs fixing

The lop lowped ower tha saaser

The flea jumped over the saucer

The plank wis se coggly 'at aa nearly tummeled off

The plank was so wobbly that I almost fell off

Theor's nowt so qweor as folk!

People are just plain weird!

They hed sic a hyem-coming as nivvor wis

You've never seen anything like their home-coming party

Thoo canna catch me   You can't catch me

Thor aa' gyen   They are all gone

Thor wis a vast o' folk i' tha chepil

The chapel was full to bursting

Thor's myekin' sic a noise aa's fair past mesel
You are making so much noise that I can't hear
  myself think
Thor's nowt to be afeared on
There's nothing to be afraid of
Thou bangs thee muthor, me canny bairn
You are better than your mother
Tyek aa swig!   Have a drink!

Ww

Wa gaanin' oot ta play   We are going out to play
Wares me ganzie?   Where is my jumper?
We knaas?   Who knows?
We've hutten wor tormits
We've harvested our turnips
Weors tha netty?   Please direct me to the toilet
Wet yer neb!   Have a drink!
Wey, thon's a canny-leukin' lass, lad
That lady looks attractive, my friend
Wh're ye coddin?   Why are you lying?
What a crop he's gi'en ye!
What sort of haircut is that?
What a neck ye hev!
You have the nerve of the Devil!
What a queer shaver he is
He's a very odd person
What are ye gaupin' at?   What are you staring at?

What are ye naggin' on at?
What are you complaining about?
What are ye sittin' clockin' theor at?
Why are you sitting for such a long time?
What cheor, hinny?   Hello, darling (to a woman)
What fettle tha day?   How are you?
What fettle, marra?   Hello, darling (to a man)
What's a marrer, marra?   What's wrong, pal?
Where are ye stoppin?   Where are you staying?
Why aye, bonny lad   Well of course, my friend
Whisht lads, haad yer gobs
Shush, boys! Stop talking
Wor lass's ganna mask tha tye
My wife is brewing the tea
Wor Nannie's a mazor   My Granny is a wonder
Wot ye dein', marra?
What are you doing, my friend?
Wrang iv his heed   Disturbed; educationally
   challenged
Wull yi luk me heed for dickies?
Will you please delouse me?

Yy

Y'alreet thun?   How are you doing?
Y'gannin' th'match th'morra?
Are you going to the football match tomorrow?
Yar aal reet, marrow   You're all right, my friend

Yar reet scabby   You're covered in spots
Yara clarty git   You're covered in mud
Ye greet lazy hoit   You great lazy lummock
Ye impitent faggit   You rude pillock
Ye mevvies misdoot me...
You perhaps doubt me...
Ye've myed a bitch on't   You have spoilt it
Yo'r varry shy wi' that baccy o' yors
I'd like a cigarette
Yu daft clot / gyet   You stupid fool

All Michael O'Mar titles are available by post from:
Bookpost, P.O. Box 29, Douglas, Isle of Man IM99 1BQ

Credit cards accepted. Please telephone 01624 836000
Fax 01624 837033
Internet http://www.bookpost.co.uk

Free postage and packing in the UK.
Overseas customers allow £1 per book (paperbacks)
And £3.00 per book (hardbacks)

Other humour titles:
The World's Stupidest Criminals – ISBN 1-85479-879-0
The World's Stupidest Men – ISBN 185479-508-2
The World's Stupidest Laws – ISBN 1-85479-549-X
The World's Stupidest Signs – ISBN 1-85479-555-4
The World's Stupidest Graffiti – ISBN 1-85479-876-6
The Book of Urban Legends – ISBN 1-85479-932-0
Outrageous Expressions – ISBN 1-85479-556-2
Totally Stupid Men – ISBN 1-85479-274-1
Stupid Men Quiz Book – ISBN 1-85479-693-3
Complete Crap – ISBN 1-85479-313-6
Wicked Cockney Rhyming Slang – ISBN 1-85479-386-1
Wicked Scouse English – ISBN 1-84317-006-X
All Men Are Bastards – ISBN 1-85479-387-X
The Ultimate Book of Farting – ISBN 1-85479-596-1
The Complete Book of Farting – ISBN 1-85479-440-X
The History of Farting –ISBN 1-85479-754-9
The Ultimate Insult – ISBN 1-85479-288-1
The Little Englander's Handbook – ISBN 1-85479-553-8